For my mother and father

Christmas

The King James Version
with pictures
by

Jan Pieńkowski

Alfred A. Knopf : New York

N THE DAYS of Herod the King,
the angel Gabriel was sent from God
unto a city named Nazareth, to a virgin
espoused to a man whose name was Joseph;

and the virgin's name was Mary.

AND THE ANGEL said,
Thou shalt bring forth a son,
and shalt call his name Jesus. He shall be called
the Son of the Highest: and of his kingdom
there shall be no end.

And Mary said, Behold the handmaid of the
Lord. And the angel departed from her.

 T CAME to pass that there went out a decree that all the world should be taxed, every one in his own city. And Joseph went up from Nazareth to the city called Bethlehem, to be taxed with Mary his wife, being great with child.

AND SHE brought forth
her firstborn son, and wrapped him
in swaddling clothes, and laid him in a manger;
because there was no room for them
in the inn.

There were in the same country shepherds
keeping watch over their flock by night.
And the angel of the Lord came upon them,
and they were sore afraid.

And the angel said unto them, Fear not:
I bring you good tidings of great joy.
For unto you is born a Saviour, which is Christ
the Lord. And this shall be a sign unto you;
ye shall find the babe wrapped in swaddling clothes,
lying in a manger.

SUDDENLY there was a multitude
of the heavenly host saying, Glory
to God in the highest, and on earth peace,
good will toward men.

THE SHEPHERDS said one to another,
Let us now go to Bethlehem.
And they found Mary, and Joseph, and the babe
lying in a manger.

And all they that heard it wondered at those
things which were told them by the shepherds.
But Mary kept all these things, and pondered them
in her heart.

And the shepherds returned, praising God.

BEHOLD, there came wise men from the east, saying, Where is he that is born King of the Jews? For we have seen his star in the east, and are come to worship him.

When Herod the King heard these things, he was troubled. And he sent them to Bethlehem, and said, Go and search diligently for the child; and when ye have found him, bring me word again, that I may come and worship him also.

WHEN THEY had heard the King, they departed; and lo, the star went before them, till it stood over where the young child was.

And they saw the young child with Mary
his mother, and fell down and worshiped him;
and when they had opened their treasures,
they presented unto him gifts:

gold, and frankincense, and myrrh.

Being warned in a dream that they should
not return to Herod, they departed into their
own country another way.

ND THE ANGEL appeared
to Joseph in a dream, saying, Arise,
and take the child and his mother, and flee
into Egypt, for Herod will seek the child
to destroy him.

When he arose, he took the child and his mother by night, and departed into Egypt.

THEN HEROD was exceeding wroth, and sent forth and slew all the children that were in Bethlehem, from two years old and under.

Then was there lamentation and weeping and great mourning.

B UT WHEN Herod was dead, an angel appeared in a dream to Joseph in Egypt, saying, Take the child and his mother, and go into the land of Israel: for they are dead which sought the young child's life.

And he took the child and his mother, and came into the land of Israel, and dwelt in Nazareth.

AND THE CHILD grew, and waxed strong in spirit, filled with wisdom: and the grace of God was upon him.

BEAUTY AND THE BEAST

Beauty and the Beast

Retold by Deborah Apy

Illustrated by Michael Hague

Holt, Rinehart and Winston

NEW YORK

This text is based on the story
by Madame Le Prince de Beaumont.

First published in 1983 by Holt, Rinehart and Winston,
383 Madison Avenue, New York, New York 10017.
Published simultaneously in Canada by Holt, Rinehart and
Winston of Canada, Limited.

Library of Congress Cataloging in Publication Data

Apy, Deborah.
Beauty and the beast.

Summary: Through her great capacity to love, a kind
and beautiful maid releases a handsome prince from the
spell which has made him an ugly beast.
[1. Fairy tales.   2. Folklore—France.]   I. Le Prince
de Beaumont, Madame (Marie), 1711–1780.   II. Hague,
Michael, ill.   III. Beauty and the beast.   IV. Title.
PZ8.A7Be 1983   398.2'1   83-4395
ISBN: 0-03-064076-8
First published by The Green Tiger Press in 1980.
Printed in the United States of America
1 3 5 7 9 10 8 6 4 2

Offset Printing and Binding: Krueger, New Berlin, Wisconsin
Composition: Waldman Graphics, Pennsauken, New Jersey

Designer: Marc Cheshire
Production Editor: Trent Duffy
Production Manager: Karen Gillis

BEAUTY AND THE BEAST

ONG AGO, IN A FAR-OFF COUNTRY, THERE LIVED A good merchant who was enormously rich. His wealth had been acquired through years of hard work, and, although his wife had died many years before, he felt greatly blessed. It was not his fortune that he counted most among his treasures, but his three daughters and three sons, whom he loved deeply. His daughters were attractive, his sons strong and robust. But of all his children, the youngest daughter was by far the most striking, and all who met her called her "Beauty."

This made the elder daughters extremely jealous. They longed for the attention that Beauty received, and made every effort to get it. They put on ridiculous airs, dressed themselves in expensive clothes, strutted before mirrors, and complimented themselves upon their appearance. When they weren't boasting of their superior qualities, they were usually complaining about something.

"Ah, Jeanette," the oldest would say to her sister, "those ostrich feathers were just what you needed for a finishing touch. What a pity that Father wouldn't order them for you."

"Yes, doesn't he get unreasonable at times? As if he had to worry about money! It's terribly unfair of him. Father should learn to recognise our station in life. Why, the other day he told me we should visit the Bruning girls, a draper's family of all things! Adelle, the colour of your gown is so becoming! We will be the very envy of the city this evening."

"Oh, Jeanette," Adelle sighed, "I am so looking forward to this ball. I hear there may even be several dukes in attendance. I would make such a marvellous duchess. You are quite right about Father. I don't know why he insists on behaving as though we were just common folk, with as little money as he had when he and Mother were first married. I mean, what does all that matter now? Sometimes he makes as little sense as that simple sister of ours."

"Really!" Jeanette laughed scornfully. "If people only knew her as we do, they wouldn't speak so highly of her. Why, just the other day I heard her simpering to Father about staying home and playing her harpsichord for him. He looked so tired. Ha! She just wants to be his favourite."

"Yes, she is shameful, I agree. And with all the reading she does, you would think she might know something about what is fashionable or current, but she's such a simple child she doesn't pay the slightest attention to being properly attired, or acquiring decent manners. She would probably curtsy to the scullery maid."

This is the way the two sisters spent their time, and they did very little to hide their condescending attitude towards Beauty. But not only was Beauty lovelier than her sisters in appearance,

she also had a much kinder and stronger character; and she paid little attention to their petty comments. Naturally, this only made her sisters meaner and angrier.

The family's great fortune attracted many eminent merchants who came to court the girls. The elder two were quick to spurn such attentions, saying they would not accept a station lower than that of a duchess, or a countess at least. Beauty was kind to those who directed themselves towards her, but told them she was too young to marry and wished to remain with her father for at least a few more years. Besides, she knew she did not feel love for them.

Suddenly, without warning, disaster struck the family. One Sunday, as they returned home from church, they discovered their house in flames. Everything burned to the ground, and they had to go to their neighbours' homes for shelter. That week, the merchant received reports that his vessels at sea were either lost to pirates or sunk in a violent storm. As he turned to his last resources, he realised that his clerks in distant countries, whom he had trusted entirely, had cheated him of his money. In just one week, the family had fallen from great wealth to dire poverty. The merchant knew he could not depend on his neighbours' generosity indefinitely. All that remained to him was a desolate cottage that stood on the northern edge of a dark forest, many miles away from the city. It was to this humble place that the family was forced to retreat.

At first, Jeanette and Adelle refused to leave. They were confident that one of their suitors would marry them, and were willing, under the circumstances, to accept a lower station than they would have considered earlier. But because they had been sought for their fortune, their lovers lost interest in them. Several gentlemen, however, wished to marry Beauty, for she had been loved for herself. But she would not abandon her father in his adversity, and was determined to go with him to the country to help as best she could.

That is not to say Beauty was not distressed. She had never worked at menial tasks before, and she was not at all sure of what to expect, nor was she sure she would be able to manage what was required of her. And the family did have to work very hard, as peasants do. They had a small dairy to mind; chickens, geese, and goats to tend; fields to farm; a family garden to care for, as well as a run-down home to maintain.

The merchant and his three sons spent all their time in the fields. Beauty rose at four in the morning to milk the cows, feed the chickens and geese, clean, cook, bake, wash, scrub, mend, and have dinner ready by the end of the day. At first it was very difficult. Beauty tired easily from the never-ending chores and longed for the luxuries of her old home. But in two months, she was healthier than ever, and she realized that she had become quite accustomed to her new life. In fact, she was happy, often singing while she worked. When her work was finished she read or played the harpsichord, which seemed to bring her even more contentment than it had when they lived in the city. The evenings became the most pleasurable time for Beauty, for it was then that her father and brothers came home for dinner, and with everyone's chores completed they could spend their time in lively conversation until they retired to bed.

Only Adelle and Jeanette could not adjust to their new life. They rose late, and spent the day crying about their plight.

Beauty's happiness and acceptance of her life only aggravated them. They mocked her for being stupid, while at the same time demanding that she see to their needs.

"Really!" Adelle cried. "I can't be expected to prepare breakfast. Get me some eggs, if that's all that we have. How can you hum as though this were a decent existence?"

"And see to it that I get some fresh milk." Jeanette added, "This milk is about to curdle."

His daughters' cruelty upset the merchant, but he was unable to do anything about it. He knew that Beauty outshone the others in spirit as well as appearance, and he wished her elder sisters possessed her industry, patience, and good nature, but he had no idea how to effect such a change. Beauty, who realised that her father blamed himself for his children's misery, had simply resolved to pay no attention to her sisters' pettiness, and to do her best to make life bearable for her father. "Oh, Beauty," the merchant would sometimes sigh late in the evening, "if only I could provide for you and your sisters so that you might all be happy."

"But, Father," Beauty would reply, "we are safe and healthy, and we have each other. There are many blessings in our life."

"I know, I know," the merchant said, "but your sisters cannot seem to live like this, and it is my fault that they have been forced to this cottage."

"Father, give them time," Beauty assured him. "It will be better."

"I just want my children to be happy."

"I know, Father," Beauty said, and kissed his brow.

Late one morning, as Beauty was carrying bread and cheese

to her brothers and father in the wheat field, there came the sound of galloping hoofbeats down the dusty road. Travellers were seldom seen in such a remote part of the country, and the sound sent a shiver of anticipation through each of them. They quickly came to the roadside to see what it was all about.

A young man pulled his sweaty horse to a halt before them. "I have travelled all the way from the city," he told them, "to let you know that one of your ships, believed lost in the storm, sailed into port several days ago. She was badly battered, but rumour has it that she still carries most of her original cargo." He cast a warm look at Beauty as he dismounted, proud of himself for being the bearer of such good news. As the family ushered him into the cottage, Adelle and Jeanette could not contain their excitement.

"Ah, finally, we shall have our brocades and jewels again," said Adelle.

"Yes, and we will return to the city," said Jeanette. "Father, you will get us a carriage, won't you?"

"Now, my children, let's see to first things first. I must go to the city, and determine just what we do have," the merchant said. But the lilt in his voice suggested that his expectations were as high as those of his elder daughters.

The next day, as he prepared to leave with the messenger, the elder sisters continued their extravagant requests. Beauty, believing in her heart that they hoped for too much, said nothing. Her father turned to her and said kindly, "Beauty, what can I bring back for you?"

Not wishing to belittle her sisters, Beauty tried to think of something to request. All she could think of was, "A rose."

"A rose?" said her father.

"Yes, I love them so, and haven't seen any in so long."

Her sisters laughed rudely, saying, "Indeed, the girl has become simpleminded in the country."

"No matter," said their father sharply. "If it is a rose that you want, a rose you shall have." With that, he mounted his horse and rode off down the dusty road.

The trip to the city was long and arduous. It took several days for the two men to reach the city, and once there, the merchant found himself faced with more troubles. The spices aboard the ship had been completely ruined in the storm; most of the silks and other valuables had been greatly damaged. As the merchant searched through the cargo, his hopes for regaining his wealth plummeted, and he worried bitterly about how he would face Jeanette and Adelle. He knew the girls were weak, and he blamed himself for having allowed them to place such high hopes on the news of the ship's recovery.

After many weeks of argument and negotiation, the merchant was left with no more than what he had carried with him to the city. What was salvageable from the ship had been claimed by creditors. His last coins were paid to the hotelkeeper as he prepared to leave for home. The pain of his disappointment was evident from the furrows of his brow. He longed to be at home with his family once again.

Although the trip to the city had been difficult, the way back was worse. The weather had changed from the mild pleasantness of summer to the unpredictable chills of autumn. As the merchant entered a gloomy part of the forest, just twenty miles from his home, a bitter storm arose. Soon the moon was black-

ened by clouds. The howling wind lashed the trees. The merchant pulled his cloak tightly around his shoulders and lowered the brim of his hat, hoping the storm would end. The poor man had no choice but to go on, for he knew he was far from any shelter, but soon he lost his way. The night grew blacker and blacker, until he could barely see the horse's mane before him. Branches scratched at the merchant's face. His bones were brittle with cold, and his skin prickled with a sense of doom. He recalled old rumours that the woods were enchanted, and feared he might never reach his children. In terror, he wandered through the evil darkness. Finally, even his heart became numb, and he was sure he would be consumed by the violent blackness. Then, suddenly, a light appeared in the distance.

With a cry of joy the merchant spurred his horse forward. Breaking through the brush, he came to a smooth, broad path, lined with orange trees, covered with flowers and fruit. Here there was no wind, and the raging storm faded away behind the perfume of flowers and singing of birds.

At the end of the path stood a magnificent castle bathed with light. Never in his life had he seen such a beautiful and awesome building. Not until he had entered the courtyard and dismounted did he notice that the castle was unnaturally silent. Not the slightest murmur was to be heard. Still, he thanked God for his good fortune and led his horse to the stable. Having unsaddled and cooled the sweating animal, he found both hay and oats for the spent creature and carried in a bucket of water. Then he turned and climbed the long steps to the castle's entrance. He entered the great hallway, and came to a startled halt.

Directly before him was a small room with a couch drawn cozily up to a warm fire. Before it stood a table set for one. "How strange!" he thought. "It is almost as if I were expected. What sort of place have I come to?" But his hunger soon overcame his fear and he ate the meal before him, hoping he might soon be able to thank his benefactor. He drank the last drop of wine in his glass. No one had yet appeared. Soon a warm drowsiness overcame him, and he fell asleep.

He was astonished to awaken in a large, comfortable bed. Fresh clothes were laid out for him, sunshine lit the room, and as he stretched and yawned he could not recall having ever felt so rested. "Surely," he mused, "this is an enchanted place." He returned to the room where he had eaten the night before and found porridge, milk, bread, and jam set out on the little table. Still, a shroud of silence hovered about him. He felt compelled to speak out. "Thank you," he said. He looked about and waited, but nothing happened.

The merchant was becoming uneasy. Anxious to continue his journey back to his family, he went to find his horse. As he descended the long flight of steps to the courtyard he noticed an arbour of roses, lovelier and more fragrant than any he had ever beheld. Remembering Beauty's request, he leaned over a hedge and picked a large red blossom. "At least," he thought, "I will be able to bring this beautiful rose to Beauty."

Instantly, he was struck with a chilling fear. Black clouds gathered, darkening the sun. Torrents of wind forced the poor man to his knees. A raven cawed in the sky. A hideous roar resounded in the merchant's ears. Trembling, he turned to see a monstrous creature rushing at him.

"Who said you might take a rose?" the creature snarled angrily. "Was it not enough that I sheltered you, fed you, and clothed you? Yet, you have the arrogance to take from me something that was not given? You shall pay for this!"

White with fear, the merchant responded, "Please, generous lord, I meant no offence. Forgive me. I am truly grateful to you. It was only for my daughter. I did not think—"

"Indeed, you did not. You have stolen a rose, and I love my roses more than anything else. I will not forgive such a trespass. You will suffer."

Almost in tears, the merchant cried out, "Suffer! But I *have* suffered. Please sire, I have lost my wife and all my possessions. All I have left in this world are my children and a poor home. I am only an old man who wishes to please his daughter, whom he has disappointed and failed too many times before."

"And your daughter," the creature asked, "she believes that you have failed her?"

"No, no," sighed the merchant. "My Beauty is lovelier and finer than your finest rose. She would never complain. Her heart has no room for thoughts of her father's failings. But I have failed her, and I only wished . . ."

The monster's gleaming eyes narrowed. His voice was cold and savage. "Your daughter then, your Beauty, who you say is more beautiful than my rose, she might save you from your fate. Go to her! If she will agree to come to me and suffer in your place, you shall be free. If not, you must return. Do not try to hide from me, either, for that is impossible."

"Beauty?" the merchant groaned. "You think I would sacrifice my Beauty? I could not, my lord. I would not—"

"Enough!" the monster roared in anger. "I am not a lord, I am a Beast, and you are to call me such. And it is your daughter, your Beauty, who is to decide if she will come to my castle. Go now. Go to her. One of you must return to me in two days. If you do not come, I will come for you."

Confused and shaken, the poor merchant watched the Beast as he angrily turned and disappeared. "Oh, dear God," the merchant cried to himself, "what have I brought upon us now? Never could I allow Beauty to come to this place. But now, if I am to die, I will at least return to my children one last time. What will become of them?"

Dejected, the merchant went in search of his horse. Finding the animal, he saddled and mounted it, and left the castle in grief.

The horse, loose-reined and without guidance, took one of the roads out of the forest, and by the day's end the good man had come to his home. As he rode through the gate, his children came running to welcome him. Adelle and Jeanette were the first to reach his side, and each was drowning out the other's questions: "Father, what has taken you so long?" "Where have you been?" "You look so tired . . . are there no other horses? A carriage?" "Where are our gifts? They must be on their way."

The tired merchant, given no chance to reply, dismounted as Beauty and her brothers reached them. "Dear Father!" Beauty said as she embraced him heartily. "We have missed you so." His tall, handsome sons hugged him and shook his hand as they started to relate the sundry details of what had passed in his absence.

Much to the dismay of all his children, the merchant looked

at them sadly with tears in his eyes. They listened in silence as he turned to Beauty and said, "Here, gentle Beauty, is your rose. But little do you know what it has cost me."

With great hesitation, Beauty reached out for the rose, which had lost neither its fragrance nor its loveliness during the journey, and lifted it to her face. "Never have I seen a flower so magnificent," she whispered. "What does this mean, Father?"

"It means, Beauty, that I am to die, for it comes from the garden of a terrible Beast who only released me so that I might see my children one last time."

Horrified at his words, his children listened as he told them his entire adventure: his dashed hopes in the city, the wild storm and grand castle, and finally the Beast and its awful demands.

"So you see, my children," the old man concluded, "we are as poor as we ever were, only now you shall have to make lives for yourselves without me. . . . I am sorry for what I have brought you to, so dreadfully sorry. . . ." Tears ran down his cheeks, and he could no longer speak.

"No, Father!" his sons exclaimed. "We will return to the Beast in your stead and destroy this ugly monster."

"No, my sons, the power of the Beast is too great. There is no chance that you could accomplish such a feat."

"But we must try—"

"No!" their father interrupted. "It would only cause even greater sorrow. I forbid it. I will return to the Beast in a day's time. There is no other way. Please, we must fill these last hours with as much pleasure as we can."

They all entered the cottage and sat down at the table. Beauty spooned out bowls of hot stew from a pot on the stove, and they ate in silence. Finally, unable to contain herself any longer, Adelle blurted out, "If only the little ninny hadn't made such a stupid request we wouldn't be in such a fix. That's what comes from putting yourself above others."

"Adelle," her father said, "please . . ."

"It's true, Father," Jeanette added. "What are we going to do now if you're no longer here?"

"Children —"

"It doesn't matter," Beauty interrupted. "Father is not going back to the Beast."

"Oh, and I suppose you are?" Adelle scoffed.

"Yes," said Beauty.

"Beauty," cried her father, "I cannot allow you to go to the Beast!"

"But Father, I must. My sisters are right. It was for me that you took the rose, and I must pay the price."

"But Beauty, you do not understand. I cannot let you go. He is too horrible and would probably kill you."

"But Father, I must go, and I will."

"No, Beauty. You are young and have a long life ahead of you. I have lived and known joy and sorrow. Now I am old and ready to die. You will not go."

"But Father, as the Beast said, it is for me to decide, not you. Surely, I would rather return to his castle than remain here and die of grief because you were gone."

"Beauty, you would defy your own father?" Anger and sadness were mixed in the merchant's voice.

"Dear Father," Beauty replied softly, "it is not right that you should go. *I* must go."

The merchant stared at his youngest daughter, then turned without replying and retired to his room. As her brothers and sisters started to speak, Beauty said to them, "Please, I cannot talk any longer just now." She began to clear the table.

Late that night, when everyone had gone to bed, Beauty sat up by the fire mending clothes. Slowly she pulled each stitch through, staring at the embers. She sighed, and set down her work. Quietly she walked to her father's bedroom door, and knocked to see if he was awake.

"Who is it?"

"It is I, Father. May I come in and talk with you?"

"Oh, Beauty. Yes. Of course." Her father opened his door. Beauty thought how old he looked, and how tired. "Father," she sighed, and embraced him.

"Beauty, I do not want you to go to the Beast. If you knew how terrible he is . . ." The merchant's voice drifted off. "Beauty, you must not go!"

"Father, I know that it is hard for you, but you are needed here. The rose was for me. I have to go."

"But what is that?" Beauty exclaimed, as her gaze fell on a trunk that she had never seen before. The chest was large, made of oak, and on the top was carved a picture of a garden. All about the garden were strange and wonderful creatures as well as the common animals of the woods: deer, rabbits, foxes, and squirrels. The loveliest of all was a small unicorn, rising on its rear legs and shaking a silky beard. The intricate carving was the work of a fine craftsman, and both Beauty and her father caught their breath as they ran their fingers over it.

"I don't know," said the merchant in astonishment. "I have

never seen such a chest in my life. I cannot imagine how it came to be here."

Carefully the merchant lifted the top of the chest. The old man and his daughter stepped back in sudden surprise. A rush of butterflies burst from the trunk. A golden light glowed from within it, and a faint melody filled the room.

"It is magic, Father. It must have something to do with the Beast."

Beauty and her father looked in the trunk and discovered silks, brocades, jewels, and pieces of silver and gold. Perfume filled the air as they took out the contents of the chest one by one and laid them on the merchant's bed.

"Here, Father, is all that my sisters asked for," said Beauty.

"Yes. It is strange, isn't it, that it should suddenly appear when we were talking about your going to the Beast's castle? I wonder what it means."

"It must mean that things are as they should be, even if we don't understand them. Don't you see, Father, this is a sign that things will be well."

"Beauty, I hope you are right. But you have not yet seen the Beast. You do not know."

"That is true, Father. But now, at least, you have some means to provide for my sisters. Please, accept the fact that I am to go to the Beast's castle."

"Beauty, you give me no choice. I do not know that it is best, but I will accede to your judgement. Only one thing. I will return to the Beast's castle with you. Once there, if you change your mind, I will be the one to stay."

"Yes, we will go together. But I will not change my mind."

"We will see, Beauty." The merchant embraced his daughter. "Just remember, I love you as much as I have ever loved anyone."

As Beauty and her father prepared to leave the next morning, her brothers again protested.

"Father, how can you forbid us from challenging this creature who would destroy our family?" they cried. "Is it right for us to sit idly while you prepare for what could be the death of both you and Beauty?"

"My sons," the merchant responded, "I know how difficult it is for you. But the Beast's power is awesome. If we tried to resist him, he would surely kill us, and then who knows what he would do to your sisters? We have no choice. I only hope that it is Beauty who returns to you, and not me."

Beauty cast a reproachful look at her father, but said nothing. Her distraught brothers paced about the cottage as she gathered together a few personal possessions. Adelle and Jeanette tried to look sad, but in their hearts they were pleased that Beauty would be gone from their lives once and for all.

Beauty cast a last look about her home. All was clean and in order, and next to the hearth was a basket of eggs gathered that morning. "There's bread and cheese," she said, "that will serve you for lunch . . . and . . . Oh, Adelle, Jeanette, and my dear brothers, I do love you." Fighting back tears, she quickly hugged and kissed them all, and hurried out the door. Outside, sleek and glistening in the sunlight, waited two magnificent horses that had arrived that morning. No sooner had the travellers mounted the horses than they were carried away at a smooth gallop.

As they lost sight of their little cottage, a warm wind arose and blew fine, soft clouds about them. The horses extended their gait and seemed to stretch into the mist, as though they were part of it. Silently, swiftly, their legs rose and fell, and soon, with the wind, they arrived at the Beast's castle.

Again this time, silence cloaked the entire grounds. Great cedars rose still and dark at the edge of green and empty lawns. The yellow afternoon sunlight drifted slowly through the leaves of ancient oaks and came to rest on crumbling stone walls.

They dismounted and the horses immediately wheeled and disappeared into the park. Beauty slipped her hand into her father's strong grasp, and gazed in awe. The castle was magnificent, yet the silence was dreadful, and she feared what might pass in the place.

"Beauty, would you—" began her father.

"Inside, Father, we should go inside," Beauty interrupted anxiously.

Together, they climbed the long flight of steps, passed the garden with its profuse display of roses, and entered the castle. Before them were lofty rooms made of many-coloured marble. Mirrors and crystal ornaments reflected the light of a thousand candles. Deep carpets of rich colours woven into intricate patterns deadened their footsteps as they walked. The polished gold flowers that adorned the tables gave evidence of human labour, but they neither saw nor heard another living being. With some difficulty the merchant found the room in which he had slept during his previous visit. Inside, there were magnificent clothes laid out for them, which fit as perfectly as if made to their measure. Hot baths lay ready for them, and having bathed and refreshed themselves, they began to feel hungry. They went to the room the merchant had first entered on the night of the storm.

As before, a fire crackled on the hearth and cast its cheerful glow about the room. On a table beautifully set with silver and exquisite crystal was laid a splendid dinner—this time for two. Beauty and her father marvelled at the selection of their favourite dishes, and the merchant could not help noting the fine wine set out for them. As they ate, Beauty could feel her spirits lifting.

"It has been a long time since I have eaten so well," she remarked. "Surely the Beast cannot be too terrible since he has provided for us like this."

"Beauty," her father cautioned, "you mustn't jump to conclusions. Who knows what the Beast's motives are? He is frightful. I still wish that you would agree to leave."

"Father, we have discussed that enough. I will not leave. Let us try to enjoy our dinner."

The merchant was hard-pressed to reply. He knew the Beast would be beyond his daughter's worst expectations, and it pained him deeply to know the horror that awaited her.

Then they heard the groaning sound of a large door opening. The Beast's slow steps echoed down the hallway. The merchant watched his daughter's face freeze in apprehension, and lamented his inability to protect her. Beauty stared, transfixed, at the entrance to the room, and her eyes widened in horror as the creature entered.

Despite all the efforts she had made to prepare herself, he was, indeed, far worse than she had imagined.

The Beast stopped. His gaze was intense and penetrating, his voice cold and grating. "Good evening, old man. Good evening, Beauty."

Trembling, Beauty stood up. "Good evening, Beast," she replied in a whisper.

"Have you come willingly?" asked the Beast. "Are you prepared to stay?"

Beauty saw the beseeching look in her father's eyes and turned away from him. Her voice was firm as she replied, "I have come willingly. I will stay."

"I am pleased," said the Beast. "As for you, old man," he continued, turning to the merchant, "you shall stay only this night. Rise quickly in the morning and take your breakfast. When the bell rings, you must depart. You will find the same horse waiting to take you home. You must never expect to see my castle again. Now, both of you are to follow me."

The Beast led them through the great hallway and down a wide, spiral staircase to a large oak door, intricately carved with some kind of indecipherable script. Turning an iron key in the lock, the Beast said to his guests, "Look within this room. Choose all that you wish to send back to your home. You will find two travelling trunks. Fill them as full as you can. It is only fitting, Beauty, that your brothers and sisters should have something precious as a remembrance of yourself." Then the Beast turned brusquely, and left them standing there.

The room was filled with astonishing riches: bolts of silks, jewels, fine perfumes, elaborate ornaments, and piles of gold. The trunks the Beast had spoken of were in the middle of the room, and as the two began to fill them they were amazed to find that the more they put into the chests, the more room there seemed to be. Finally, they were so heavy that even an elephant could not have moved them.

"The Beast mocks us!" said the merchant. "He must know I could never carry these away."

"We can only wait and see," answered Beauty. "Let us fasten them up and leave them ready."

When they had completed their task, there were enough riches in the chests to ensure that the merchant and his family would be rich again. As Beauty laid a last silk dress across the top of the chest, she said, "There, Father. Surely Adelle and Jeanette will be satisfied with this."

"Who knows, Beauty, what your sisters will say, though no doubt they should be satisfied. Most likely they will wish to return to the city, but I think not. We will stay in our cottage until you come back to us. Oh, Beauty. . . ."

"Yes, Father," Beauty said quickly, "someday we will be together again."

They retraced their steps up the winding staircase to their room, where two large, comfortable beds had been turned down for them. Despite their weariness, Beauty and her father did not expect to sleep. But they had scarcely lain down when they fell fast asleep. As she slept, Beauty dreamed.

In her dream she was standing in a fragrant garden, and a fine lady in a gossamer dress came towards her. At the lady's side pranced a small, delicate unicorn with shining eyes. It seemed that Beauty and the lady knew each other well, and the lady knew that Beauty's heart was full of confusion and fear. She spoke, saying, "Beauty, I am content with your goodwill.

Do not abandon your kind ways in fear. In your heart, you know what is right. Trust your heart, and search out the truth. But beware of being deceived by appearances. Bear the trials to come, and your goodness will be rewarded."

Upon waking, Beauty spoke of the dream to her father, and it seemed to comfort him. Despite the Beast's words, the merchant cherished a hope that he might be able to return to Beauty soon, or that somehow he would see her again, and he ate his breakfast with a good appetite. But Beauty, for all her bravado, was sure that her father was leaving forever and that she would never see him again. When the bell rang sharply, it pierced her very heart.

When they reached the courtyard, they found two horses waiting, one loaded with the two chests and the other saddled for the merchant. The Beast was nowhere to be seen.

"At least," Beauty said, "the Beast has kept his word about the trunks."

The merchant embraced his daughter. "Oh, Beauty . . ." he said with pain in his voice.

The two looked at each other, but neither could speak another word. When the merchant had mounted, the horses set off at such a pace that Beauty lost sight of him immediately.

She uttered a sharp cry. Tears streamed down her face. The immense loneliness of the castle, the loss of everything familiar, and her fear of the Beast closed upon her. "What am I to do?" she moaned to herself. She wandered aimlessly about the castle grounds, wrapped in the awful silence, seeing nothing before her. Now she was alone, and frightened. Totally exhausted, she reentered the castle. Sinking to the couch in the room where she had eaten with her father such a short while ago, she noticed a glass of amber liquid.

She lifted it to her lips and sipped. The drink was cool and soothing, and with relief she drank all that was there. Gradually, she felt rested and less fearful. "I suppose," she mused, "I might as well see what is here." She rose and began to explore her new dwelling.

The castle was magnificent, each room more dazzling then the last. Beauty was taken aback when she came to a door over which was written "Beauty's Chamber." She opened it hastily and beheld a marvellous room. There were many books, a harpsichord, and a cabinet of music. A feather bed was covered with silk sheets and comforters. On the head of the bed was carved a bold, beautiful unicorn. Climbing roses were twined about the trellis outside the window, and sunlight poured into the room. Beauty was cheered, and taking a book from the shelves, she opened it to the following words:

> In this house your will shall be
> Vested with authority.
> Speak thy wish and you shall wear
> Garments without seam or tear.

"Oh my!" gasped Beauty, shutting the book. She sat down before a beautiful vanity, above which hung a large looking glass. At the top of the glass were written the words "Reflect for Me," and, at the bottom, the words "I Will Reflect for You." Beauty held her head in her hands, shaken by all the surprises of the day, and sighed, "My dear father, are you all right? If only I could see you again." And even as she was speaking, she lifted her eyes to the mirror and was astonished to see the image of her father arriving home, worn and dejected, but safe. Her brothers and sisters were there to greet him. A moment later, the image disappeared.

Beauty held her breath. What enchantment was it that held this place? Confused, but reassured by the seeming kindnesses of the Beast, she continued her exploration.

Opening a door that led from her room, she was faced with what seemed to be an immense, empty hall, dark and dusty with but a few glimmering lights at the far end. With uncertain steps, she entered, her eyes slowly adjusting to the unfamiliar dimness.

Suddenly, she heard the loud rush of many wings flapping about her. Startled, Beauty threw up her arms for protection and drew back. The light grew brighter, revealing an enormous flock of exotic birds. Peacocks, parrots, and cockatoos glided about. Warblers and doves cooed and chirped melodiously. The sight was magnificent, and Beauty was enthralled. "This is beautiful," she thought, and contentedly sat down on a wide ledge. A thrush alighted on her shoulders, bursting with repetitions of his song. "Never," thought Beauty, "had I imagined such loveliness would be found here, or that I should feel so peaceful."

After some time, Beauty decided to see what other surprises the castle held for her. She rose and opened the door to the next room. Here, the walls were lined with mirrors, and many chairs were placed in the center, facing outwards. As she sat down in the first chair, she was astonished to see an amusing

pantomime being acted for her. She got up and went from chair to chair, and found, reflected in all the mirrors, wonderful plays and dances, accompanied by music and coloured lights. The entertainment continued, changing as Beauty changed her chairs, amusing her for many hours.

As day turned to dusk, Beauty returned to her room and found an elegant gown laid out for her. She had seen no evidence of the Beast the entire day, and as she descended for dinner she was surprised to find a place set for only one. She ate her dinner, which she found delicious, and it was only when she had finished that she heard the noise of the Beast.

She could not stop the apprehension that rose within her as the monster approached. All memory of the loveliness she had seen that day vanished. The monster was grim and ugly, and she trembled as he drew closer.

"Good evening, Beauty," said the Beast.

"Good evening," she replied, almost inaudibly. She tried to look at the Beast, but she could not hold his gaze.

"Might I stay and talk with you?" he asked.

"Well, yes, of course, if that is what you wish."

"Beauty, it is not what *I* wish, but what *you* wish that matters. This is your castle now. You are to be mistress here. You need but bid me leave, and I will obey, immediately. You think me terribly ugly, do you not?"

The Beast's stare was so intense that Beauty felt herself flush with confusion, and could barely reply, "Yes, that is true."

"Ah." The Beast's sigh was long and heavy. "I know. It is true. And I am simple, besides. How foolish my hopes and desires are. I am a stupid, horrible creature."

Beauty glanced at the Beast. His huge, hairy chest rose and fell in deep sighs. Mixed with her fear, she felt, for the first time, compassion for her captor.

"But, Beast, even if this is true, you have been kind and generous. Everything I have thought or wished for has been satisfied instantly. I believe you are very good-natured. Truly, when I consider these things, your deformities grow less."

"It is true," said the Beast, "that inside this rough skin I have a loving heart. I am sorry to bring you to this place. Your goodness, the willingness with which you sacrificed yourself for your father's sake, makes me almost ashamed. Trust that my need for you is very great. I cannot tell you more than that. But, Beauty, do not be afraid of me. I see your virtue and do homage to it. I am your servant, not your master. Only ask, and anything within my power to give is yours."

The Beast paused and, after gazing at her for a moment in silence, bowed his head and continued softly, "Perhaps in time you will no longer see my ugliness. Perhaps . . . perhaps . . . But, still . . ." And here Beauty saw his shoulders bend as though under a great weight and his face twist with anguish. "Still," he cried, raising his hairy paws before his face, "I am a monster! Not only is my body misshapen but the beast rides my spirit as well. Oh, my Beauty, little do you know of me! And, even knowing little, you cannot help but see me as monstrous! It is hopeless!"

Beauty trembled, and wondered how long the Beast meant to keep her there, and what he would do next. The Beast saw her fear.

"Don't be afraid," he said.

Wide-eyed, she simply nodded her head.

"Beauty"—his voice was softer, though still coarse—"might I come to visit with you in the evenings, when you have finished dining?"

"Yes," she said, "but when do you dine? Why do you come only when I am finished?"

For the first time, the Beast's eyes evaded Beauty's glance, and he simply answered, "That is how it should be." His next words sent a chill through her. "Beauty, will you be my wife?"

It was some time before she dared answer him. She sat with her face turned away from him, struggling to master her feelings of shock and repulsion. She feared angering him. At last, she managed to say softly, "No, I cannot."

Immediately he choked and groaned so frightfully that the whole castle echoed with his grief. Beauty was dismayed at the effect of her refusal, but she began to recover from her fright as soon as she realised that the Beast was not angry with her. After a time, he merely said, in a sorrowful voice, "Farewell then, Beauty," and left the room with heavy tread and many backward, longing glances at her.

Beauty was relieved to be alone again. This first real encounter with the Beast had been very trying and not a little alarming. Soon, however, she began to feel compassion for him. "Alas," she thought, "poor creature. How terrible it must be for him to be so very ugly." Still, as she returned to her room, she could not help but be thankful that the Beast apparently did not intend to press himself upon her often.

Beauty found it difficult to endure her first days at the Beast's castle. Consumed by loneliness and concern for her family's welfare, she passed the time wandering disconsolately from room to room. In the course of these wanderings she discovered a library in which it seemed that books had been selected and laid out with her interests in mind. They had beautiful pictures, and she felt they had a meaning that she could not grasp. And, strangest of all, when she returned to the library she could never find the exact pictures and words that she had puzzled over the day before. They were similar, but not the same. It almost seemed as if they lived and moved until they were frozen by her gaze.

Wonders such as the library were not the only evidence Beauty had of the Beast's concern for her happiness and entertainment. Every comfort and luxury was available to her. A changing array of jewels and perfumes appeared in her dressing room, though by what hands she never saw. Her favourite foods were prepared for her meals and her favourite flowers mysteriously appeared in the garden. The Beast told her to pick all she liked and she filled her room with them. Their cheerful, fragrant faces seemed like friends from her old life, and comforted her.

Still, she could not keep from dreading the Beast's arrival every evening after dinner. She feared his bestiality, at any moment, might break the restraints under which he kept himself. After a few days, however, she came to know that although he asked, each evening, the awful question, "Beauty, will you be my wife?" with passion trembling behind his voice, he always accepted her refusal without anger.

His sadness and his quiet resignation to the pain of this rejection touched Beauty's gentle heart and greatly lessened her repugnance for him. With each visit his singular appearance seemed less fearsome. More and more she felt that his rough voice and movements did not altogether reflect his heart and spirit.

One evening, after she had been at the castle some time, Beauty noticed that the Beast was disturbed and restless when he came to see her after dinner. He made his usual polite inquiries after her well-being and happiness, but he seemed distracted. Beauty tried to engage him by asking him about the castle and about the wonderful things she had found there.

"Tell me," said Beauty, "did you select the books in your library and do you ever read them? I do not understand the books I read there. It is as if they hold a message that I cannot quite find."

But all the Beast would say was, "Yes, Beauty, I made the library," and retreat again into his troubled reverie.

At length the Beast heaved a great sigh and stood up. He stared at Beauty in silence, with a look that mingled pain, longing, and despair. It made her very uncomfortable. Then he made his nightly request for her hand in marriage and upon her refusal turned at once and strode quickly from the room, with only a murmured, "Good night, Beauty. Sleep soundly."

Later, in her room, Beauty turned down the lamps and, thinking the air oppressively warm, opened the casement that overlooked the park. The wind blew softly. The night air was fresh and cool. She thought of the Beast and of his terrible sadness. With a deep sigh, she lay down in her bed and began to sleep.

Suddenly, a sharp cry pierced the air. Beauty sat upright,

fear racing through her. Her heart pounded as she heard the cry again . . . a loud, sharp shriek and then a long moan that seemed to last forever. Finally, it stopped. Beauty sat in her bed a long time, unable to move. Finally, she fell asleep, wondering what it was that had just died.

That night, when she was sleeping, the door to her room opened slowly, and the Beast entered. He went from her to the window, which he quickly shut and locked. Then the Beast walked to the side of Beauty's bed and looked at her longingly. He stood this way, for many hours, blood dripping from his hands.

Beauty woke the next morning, disturbed and unrested. The room was very hot, and when she glanced towards the window, she was surprised to find it closed and locked. She wondered uneasily who had entered while she slept. Since there was no one to question, she tried to dismiss her fears and rose from her bed. She stood before her mirror brushing her long hair. Her eye caught the pictures embroidered on the curtains of her bed, and she was suddenly reminded of her dream.

In the night she had seemed to wake, and as she lay there it seemed that her bed was surrounded by a mist. Out of this haze appeared the same beautiful fairylike lady who had come to her before. The lady said, "Arise," and grasping Beauty's hand, she led her through a maze of corridors into a large meadow surrounded by hedges that towered above her head. Then the fairy said to her, "Dear Beauty, do not long for that which you have left behind. You are destined for a better fate. Only do not be deceived by appearances." Then the lady disappeared, and Beauty was left standing alone.

She wandered in confusion between the hedgerows and saw a handsome prince approaching her. At his side walked the unicorn she had seen before with the fairy. "Beauty, Beauty," cried the handsome man, "you are too cruel. Will you ever see me? I fear not! Look with your heart, I beg you. Do not be deceived by your eyes. Be as true-hearted as you are beautiful, and you will find me out. Please, do not desert me, but save me from my suffering." The young man stared at her with a piercing gaze, until finally the unicorn stamped its foot and the dream was over.

"Oh, my," sighed Beauty. "Such strange visions. What could be the meaning of them? It unsettles me. I don't understand. But, they are only dreams . . . why should I trouble myself so with them?" Still, she could not help feeling that somehow it was her fault.

Whatever guilt she felt, however, was gradually forgotten. She spent three months very contentedly in the castle. And she dreamed no more, for which she was grateful. Her days belonged to her alone, and she was always finding new sources of entertainment in her new home. Occasionally, something would occur to jar the memory of her dreams, as once, when she entered a large gallery of paintings, she saw a portrait resembling the man in her dreams. It startled her, and made her wonder. But then she decided it was probably her imagination. The portrait simply reminded her of someone she had seen long ago. But Beauty did not return to the gallery, for the memory of her dreams made her uncomfortable.

Beauty never met the Beast during the day. She was in the habit of walking in the park late in the afternoon when the air was cool and the light slanted peacefully through the trees. Occasionally, when the sun was setting, she would catch a glimpse of the Beast standing atop a high hill and looking off into the distance. But then he would quickly disappear, and it was only in the evenings that she spoke with him.

She had come to anticipate the Beast's visits with pleasure. With all that there was for her to do in the castle, she nonetheless was lonely. Usually by early afternoon, she found herself thinking of the Beast. He was no longer fearsome to her; in fact, she thought he was very amiable. Seeing him so often had accustomed her to his ugliness, so that she hardly noticed it. He always talked with plain good sense, and she enjoyed their conversations. One evening, when the Beast spoke disparagingly of himself, Beauty quickly came to his defence.

"Really, Beast," she said, "among men there are many who are far more monstrous than you. I prefer you to those who, under a fair form, hide a treacherous, ungrateful heart."

"Beauty," he replied, "do you really mean that?"

"Why, yes, of course, or else I would not have said it. My dear Beast, you have many fine qualities. You are honest and just; you are always true to your word. You are thoughtful and kind to me, and, despite your appearance, you are most gentle." She smiled warmly at him, heartened by her own speech and wanting to make him happy. "Truly, Beast, I think very highly of you."

The Beast rose from his seat and bowed low before Beauty. "Beauty, you are kind," he said solemnly. "Would you come with me to the balcony?"

"Certainly, but why?"

"Simply for the pleasure of it," he said. "Come with me." With a bold turn he strode from the room.

Beauty followed him through the opened doors out into the night. The air was sweet, for the Beast's roses always seemed most fragrant in the evening. The stars sparkled in the night sky, and a pale sliver of moon hung on the horizon. The warm breeze caressed her cheeks, and moved her hair about her face.

"It is lovely," she said. Since she arrived at the enchanted castle she had seldom been outside during the night.

"Beauty," said the Beast in a low voice, "would you give me the pleasure of dancing with me?"

Beauty hesitated. She looked from his huge, hairy arms to his awkward feet, and then to his deep-set eyes that watched her tenderly. Affection for him swept over her, and she gracefully bowed her head and said, "Yes, I would be happy to."

The Beast extended his arm to her, and as she reached to take it a wonderful melody filled the air. Firmly, lightly, the creature danced with her, gently guiding her across the balcony. Beauty was astonished at the skill of his movement, the strength of his grasp and tenderness of his touch. She closed her eyes and released herself. Her heart pounded, and she was filled with an inexpressible happiness.

"What a lovely night," she sighed, as they finally stopped to rest by the marble banister.

"Beauty"—the Beast's gaze was as intent as it had ever been—"will you be my wife?"

"Oh no!" she cried. "I am sorry. I wish I could consent to be your wife, but I will not deceive you. No. No! I simply couldn't." Flustered and confused, Beauty hurried back indoors with the

Beast behind her. "Of course," she continued, "you will always be my friend. Why does that not satisfy you?"

"Beauty," the Beast sighed, "I value whatever you will give me. That you offer me your friendship is more than I ever should have hoped for, and you cannot know what pleasure that gives me." Yet the creature's eyes were filled with sorrow, and he seemed to struggle to contain a deep, groaning growl that could not be altogether quieted. He left abruptly and Beauty retired to her room, but she did not sleep well that night, for her heart was troubled.

The next day, as she walked about, Beauty discovered a gate on the castle grounds that she had never seen before. It was overgrown with weeds, and the iron lock that secured it was old and rusty. Glancing down, she spied a key lying on a step nearby that opened the lock when she tried it. The hinges creaked as she pushed against the gate, and it took some effort to open it sufficiently to pass through.

Beyond the gate, Beauty was amazed to discover a vast garden that must once have been magnificent. On one hand were formal gardens in which Nature had long had her way. No recent gardener's shears had kept the lines and curves in shape, and Beauty laughed to see a pair of boxwood swans sprouting bushy antlers and tail feathers. In the other direction had apparently been the flower and statuary garden. Cultivated flowers had gone wild and now lounged in riotous confusion with their wild cousins. Yarrow and mint scented the air. But the thing that made Beauty hold her breath was the wildlife — rabbits, deer, squirrels, goats — every creature imaginable moved in peaceful harmony. Beauty was enchanted. She moved cau-

tiously towards a rabbit and was delighted to find it unafraid of her touch. Then, as she knelt to stroke a small fawn, she glimpsed a shimmering creature, small and delicate, tossing a silky forelock about a whorled horn. Quickly she rose to follow it. As she approached a crumbling statue of the god Pan, she noticed an inscription carved in the base. She walked up close to it, and ran her fingers along the carved letters, which read:

Seek within
To wisdom gain;
Thus relieve
All worldly pain.

Beauty stared. Her mind ached. She read the words again. She looked around for the strange animal she had been following, but could see no trace of it. It seemed there was something here she was to learn, but whatever it was, it was too obscure. She longed for things to become clear to her, but she did not understand.

That night she spoke to the Beast about the garden, but he only sighed and said, "Beauty, I am sorry but I cannot explain it to you." And though she persisted in her questions, he would not discuss it.

Beauty did not return to the garden again. At first she thought of it often, but whenever she came to the gate, the key that opened it was nowhere to be found, and so there was no way that she might enter. Finally, in frustration, she banged her fists against the heavy gate, as though some magical door-man might appear. Nothing happened. After a while she decided to forget about the whole matter, and tried to turn her mind to less troublesome things.

At first, it seemed to work. The days blended one into the next. Beauty was quite content, until one day she cast her eyes on the magic looking glass and was dismayed at what it revealed. In it she saw her father, who was sick, weaker and more frail than she had ever seen him. He seemed to have aged many years in the few months she had been with the Beast, and she was shocked at his appearance. "Oh, dear," she said, "I must go to him. But how will I ever get the Beast to allow it? He has been good to me, but . . . I must try." She decided to speak to the Beast after dinner that night.

"What is wrong, Beauty?" the Beast asked, noting her anxiety, as he seemed to sense all of her moods.

"There is something I must ask you," she said. "Something terrible has happened, and . . ."

"Yes? What is it, Beauty?"

Beauty paused and looked at the monster. She was hesitant, for she knew that he would respond grievously, and she wished neither to anger nor to hurt him.

"It is my father. I saw him in the mirror, terribly ill, and it is all from grief over me. If I could only go to see him, I know it would help him. . . ."

Upon hearing this, the Beast cried miserably, "Ah, Beauty, would you desert me so easily?"

"Oh, no! I would not desert you. . . . But my father may die without me. . . ."

"As I shall, Beauty."

Beauty blushed painfully at his words, knowing she was

causing him great anguish. "Dear friend," she said softly, "I could not forsake you. Only let me go to visit my poor father. I will return. But I do so long to see him now."

"I would rather die than cause you grief," said the monster. "I will send you home; you shall remain with your father, and poor I will perish of loneliness."

"No," cried Beauty, "I could not bear to cause your death. I promise to return in a week. Suffer me one week with my father, so he may know that I am well."

The Beast, who had been sighing deeply as she spoke, replied, "I cannot refuse anything you ask, though it may cost me my life. Tomorrow morning you shall be with your father. But do not forget your vow, and return in one week. If you do not come back in good time, you will find your faithful Beast dead. Now take this ring. When you are ready to come back, turn it around your finger and say firmly, 'I wish to go back to my castle and see my Beast again.' Good night, Beauty. Fear nothing and sleep peacefully, for when you awake you shall be with your father once more." Saying this, the Beast turned around and sadly left the room.

Beauty looked at the ring the Beast had given her. It was heavy and ornate and seemed rather ugly to her. But it slipped easily onto her finger, and, once in place, seemed smoother and lighter than it had in her hand. "How peculiar," Beauty thought as she went to bed. But in her excitement over going home she soon forgot about the ring. When she finally fell asleep, she began to dream.

It was the fairy again, and she seemed to be looking at Beauty with great concern. Beauty tried to reassure her, but no words would come from her mouth. The lady motioned to Beauty, who rose and followed her. Beauty was surprised to find herself alone in Pan's garden. She sat down on a tree stump, and heard a noise behind her. It was the unicorn, its eyes filled with tears. Beauty opened her arms and embraced the small creature. She could sense the sorrow coursing through its slender body. Softly, she stroked its neck. The unicorn gently laid its head in her lap, and her heart was filled with such sweetness and sadness that Beauty was utterly bewildered. Then everything faded into darkness.

When she awoke, she found herself in bed, at her father's house. As she sat up, the maid entered the room, and with a shriek of surprise, ran to tell the merchant. The good man hurried up the stairs and was nearly overcome with shock at the sight of his dear daughter.

"Beauty! Beauty!" he cried, embracing her joyfully. Tears of happiness streamed down his cheeks. "Beauty, I had given up hope of ever seeing you again. How did you escape? Beauty, what a joy to see you."

She threw her arms around him, crying and laughing in happiness. "Father," she said. "My dear, dear father."

"Come, Beauty. Sit down. Tell me, what happened? Are you all right? Were you safe from that horrible creature?"

"Yes, yes, Father. I am fine. And the Beast is not a horrible creature. He is actually kind and gentle. And I did not escape. It was he who brought me here. He let me come."

"He released you? You're here to stay?"

"Well, no, not exactly. I must return in a week."

"Return? But Beauty, you mustn't! Not now, not when

you've just come back. I have missed you so."

"Oh, Father, I have missed you, too. The Beast allowed me to come because I have missed you, and knew that you were sick." The merchant looked at her in surprise. "Yes, you see I know what has happened here. The Beast has let me know. Truly, Father, he wants me to be happy."

"If he wanted you to be happy, he would let you stay in your home where you belong."

"Father, let us worry about it later. Now I am here with you, and it is wonderful to be home again."

"Yes, Beauty, you are right. Come now, get dressed and come downstairs. We can sit together, and you can tell me about everything that has happened since I left you at that castle. How I have grieved since that day! And now I understand that strange trunk! Of course, it is yours." Beauty looked at her father curiously. "A trunk arrived earlier this morning," he explained, "or, I should say, appeared rather strangely. No one here could open it. But now I understand. It must be yours, from the Beast." The merchant ordered the trunk brought up, and Beauty easily opened it. Inside were many new dresses, as magnificent as the ones she wore at the enchanted castle. Choosing the plainest dress she could find, Beauty decided she would give the others to her sisters. But no sooner had she spoken than the trunk vanished.

"My, Beauty," said her father, "your Beast is a strange creature. But clearly, he wishes these dresses for you alone. You had best keep them to yourself." And even as he said the words, the trunk reappeared.

As Beauty was dressing, her sisters arrived at the cottage

with their husbands. The large dowries made possible by the treasure chests that the merchant had brought home moved several men to court Beauty's older sisters. Jeanette had married a man who was very handsome, but so fond of himself that he neglected everyone else, including his wife. Adelle had married a wit who used his gift to bedevil everyone, most of all his wife. The merchant could barely tolerate his sons-in-law, but he realised his elder daughters had reaped what they had sown. Little had changed in their hearts, despite their opportunities, and when Adelle and Jeanette beheld Beauty, adorned in royal clothes and lovelier than ever, they sickened with envy. As she told them of the marvellous castle and of her happiness, they could barely stifle their jealousy.

Saying they wished to recover from their surprise with a breath of fresh air, the two sisters retired to the garden venting their anger and frustration in bitter words.

"How unfair!" Jeanette ranted. "How terribly unfair that that disgusting little creature should be so much happier than ourselves!"

"Did you hear her? Did you hear all the wonderful things that she has at her disposal? And the little hypocrite says, 'But I've missed you so.' I can't bear it!" Adelle cried.

"And the Beast, she barely ever sees him. He doesn't bother her in the least. All she has to do is talk to him for a few minutes at night. So what? It's just not right. She has always been so much more fortunate than we."

"Sister"—Adelle's voice dropped to a whisper—"a thought occurs to me. What if we were to keep the little witch for more than her allotted week? Perhaps it would so enrage that ugly

monster of hers that he will take everything away from her, and it will be her turn to envy us."

Jeanette smiled. "Yes," she replied, "it is time for her to suffer. We must show her as much kindness as we can, and she will forget about leaving. Then we will see what happens."

When they returned, they lavished such attention upon her that Beauty wept with happiness. Although she had always seemed to ignore her sisters' cruelty, in truth it had hurt her deeply, and she was more than happy to believe they had had a change of heart. "Perhaps," she thought, "it is because I have been gone, or maybe it is my dear Beast's magic again. . . . Oh, I don't know, but how good it is to be loved by my sisters."

The week passed swiftly. Every day, Adelle and Jeanette came to visit Beauty, took her for rides in their carriages, entertained her in their homes, and arranged for her to meet their many new friends, some of whom were eligible bachelors who had heard of Beauty's loveliness. Beauty was swept up in all the activity and, although at times the ring hung heavy on her finger, she enjoyed herself. But what pleased her most was simply to sit and talk with her father. Every evening after dinner, the two of them would draw their chairs before the fire, and engage in long, warm conversations.

One evening, as the time for Beauty's departure was drawing close, her father spoke again of the Beast. "Beauty," he asked, "are you sure that you wish to return to the Beast? It must be very frightening for you."

"At first it was. Indeed, I would tremble every time he came into the room. But Father, he is so gentle. He would never harm me. And after a while I found I really enjoyed talking to him. Sometimes he's funny and makes me laugh. Other times, though, he seems so very sad that I must turn away from him so as not to cry myself. I only wish he would not always ask me to marry him."

Her father looked shocked. "Surely, Beauty, you would not consent to marry a monster?"

"Really, Father, he is not the monster he appears to be. Certain forces obey him, others command him, and he struggles greatly. It is he who suffers the most."

"You pity him, then?"

"It is more than pity, although that is what I felt at first. I don't know if I can explain it. Also, he seems to need me, but it is more than that."

"Beauty, you will suffer for being so good."

"Father, this monster is good." Tears welled up in Beauty's eyes, and she thought longingly of her Beast, for she knew he missed her, and she missed him.

The next day was to be Beauty's last at her father's home, and her sisters arrived early in the morning. Their eyes were red and puffed-up, and Beauty was alarmed when she saw them. "Good heavens," she cried, "what is wrong?"

"Oh, Beauty," Jeanette wept, "we are simply heartbroken that you are leaving. It is as though we are only now coming to understand each other, and love each other, and we wish you would stay for just a few more days."

"Beauty, wouldn't you consider just another day or two? Surely, your Beast would understand. And Father needs you, too. It would not be forever, Beauty. . . . We know you must go back. But just a day or two. We need you here."

Beauty looked from Jeanette to Adelle, and then thought of her dear father. "Well," she said uneasily, "I suppose, just a day. The Beast would understand one day. . . ."

And so, Beauty agreed to stay with them. The next day they convinced her to do the same, and the next. She noticed that the ring she wore on her finger had become painfully heavy, but she continued to push the thought of the Beast from her mind. Then, on the tenth night, she had a frightening dream.

Out of a very black night came the fairy, in a shimmering dress that flashed with streaks of lightning. She stared at Beauty, and then began to disappear, growing smaller and smaller until she had utterly vanished. Beauty cried out, and then heard thundering hoofbeats behind her. She turned to see the unicorn, grown and magnificent, leaving a trail of sparks as he galloped swiftly back and forth. Then he, too, disappeared into the void, and Beauty was alone. Suddenly, she found herself in the castle garden. From behind some bushes she heard painful groans. "What's that?" she cried fearfully, running down a stone path. There, behind the bushes, was the Beast, in the agony of death. He looked at her reproachfully, saying, "Beauty, why have you treated me so? Why have you broken your word? Why have you broken my heart?" And then he spoke no more.

Beauty started out of her sleep and burst into tears. "What have I done to my dear Beast?" she cried. "How could I have listened to my sisters? He is so kind and good . . . and though he is ugly, how could he be blamed for that? I have been so blind. Have I killed him? How wicked I am. I cannot stand it! My dear Beast, who is sweeter and more virtuous than anyone I have ever known."

Beauty quickly plucked a rose from a window vine and placed it in a vase for her father, hoping he would understand why she had gone. Then she turned the ring and said firmly, "I wish to go back to my castle and see my Beast again."

Immediately, she fell asleep. When she awoke it was morning and she was in her room at the Beast's castle. Everything was there as before—her books and instruments, the birds, the roses and gardens, all her possessions and memories—and she was happy and relieved to be there again. Still, the day seemed tediously long as she waited for dinner and her appointed hour with the Beast. Selecting her finest gown, she dressed, and was flushed with excitement as the clock struck nine.

Yet when the last chime faded, no Beast had arrived. "Where is he?" Beauty murmured. "Why is he late?" As the minutes ticked by, she became increasingly frightened by his absence. Finally, in despair, she left the room to search the castle. She rushed from room to room, but he was nowhere to be found.

Beauty ran from the castle out into the grounds. Past the rose bushes, up and down the paths she flew, calling for him in vain. The silence of the castle, to which she had grown accustomed, seemed to mock her now. Exhausted, she sank to the ground, and began to sob.

Then she raised her eyes, and saw before her the pathway from her dream. She instantly rose and flew down the path, calling "Beast, dear Beast, where are you?" Then, suddenly she found him, lying still and quiet upon the ground, seemingly dead.

In despair, Beauty fell to the ground beside him, weeping bitterly.

She lifted his heavy head and laid it gently in her lap. "Oh, my Beast," she cried. "What have I done to you?" She stroked his hairy face, and the tears from her eyes fell to his cheeks.

Slowly, the Beast's eyes opened. His voice was faint and faltering. "Beauty, have you come back to me?"

Her heart pounded. "Beast . . . dear, dear Beast. Yes. Please, do not die. I love you. Live for my sake; from this moment I vow to be your wife. I could not bear to be without you."

No sooner were these words spoken than fireworks exploded in the sky, and the sound of beautiful music filled the air.

Beauty looked up, dazed. Her eyes darted from the castle to the sky, and her mind raced in confusion. Turning to the Beast, she drew back in shock from the sight that greeted her. Beast was gone, and before her stood the handsome prince of her dreams.

"Where is my Beast?" she gasped.

"Before you, Beauty," said the prince. "I was the Beast. Many years ago, a wicked fairy condemned me to remain in that shape until a beautiful woman would consent to marry me. I could not reveal my plight to her. Of all souls only you were generous enough to see me as I am, and selfless enough to devote your life to me. Your understanding and virtue and love are beyond compare. Beauty, I love you deeply, and all I have I give to you."

As the meaning of what the prince said became clear, joy flooded Beauty's heart, and she held out her hand to him. Tenderly, the prince kissed it and lifted her to her feet. "My true Beauty," he said as he took her in his arms. Beauty's eyes shone with happiness as she returned his kiss and stroked the shining hair that had so miraculously replaced the Beast's rough mane. Then, hand in hand, they walked back to the castle.

There, in the great hall, Beauty was delighted to find her father and the entire family, looking somewhat bewildered. Accompanying them was the lady of Beauty's dreams. By her side pranced the unicorn, its nostrils flared with excitement.

"I have watched over you," said the lady, "for I, too, am a fairy. Although I could not alter the acts of my wicked sister, because of your virtue, I am able to use my powers once again. You have trusted your heart and deserve a reward. I will make the prince the king of his land and you shall be his queen."

Then the fairy addressed herself to Beauty's father. "My good man," she said, "you have been devoted to your children all of your life, and although you have not always made the best decisions, your good intentions and integrity have brought you to this final reward. It is your happy fate to spend the rest of your days in comfort and happiness with your daughter and her husband. You shall be blessed with the joy of many grand-children, and the peace and contentment that come from having lived your life with honour and integrity."

Turning to Adelle and Jeanette, who had been stunned into complete silence, the fairy continued, "As for you, vain ladies, I know your wicked hearts. You shall both become statues, yet alive within the stone. It will be your punishment to stand before your sister's gate and behold her happiness. Not until you have honestly acknowledged your faults will you be able to return to natural states. But I fear you will never repent. Pride, anger, selfishness, and idleness are sometimes conquered, but

the conversion of a cruel and envious mind can only be accomplished by a miracle."

With a wave of her wand the fairy transported all who were in the hall to the prince's dominions, where his subjects received him with joy. He married Beauty, and they lived happily ever after.

Only the unicorn remained on the magical grounds of the Beast's castle. And it is said that, for countless years, all who stumbled upon that place in despair were changed upon their departure, and that subsequently their fortunes were enhanced, and their hearts were filled with goodness and beauty.